We're from

Greece

Victoria Parker

Welcome
to Greece!

Heinemann Library
Chicago, Illinois

© 2005 Heinemann Library
a division of Reed Elsevier Inc.
Chicago, Illinois

Customer Service 888-454-2279
Visit our website at www.heinemannlibrary.com

Photo research by Maria Joannou
Photography by Fiona Freund
Designed by Ron Kamen and Celia Jones
Printed and bound in China by South China Printing Company

09 08 07 06 05
10 9 8 7 6 5 4 3 2 1

Library of Congress Cataloging-in-Publication Data
Parker, Victoria.
  We're from Greece / Victoria Parker.
     p. cm. -- (We're from ...)
  Includes bibliographical references and index.
  ISBN 1-4034-5784-0 (Lib. Binding-hardcover) -- ISBN 1-4034-5791-3 (pbk.) 1. Greece--Social life and customs--1974---Juvenile literature. 2. Children--Greece--Juvenile literature. 3. Family--Greece--Juvenile literature. I. Title. II. Series: We're from.
  DF854.P418 2005
  949.507'6--dc22

                              2004018476

Acknowledgments
The author and publisher are grateful to the following for permission to reproduce copyright material:
Corbis/Royalty Free pp. 4a. 4b. 30b; European Central Bank p. 30a; Fiona Freund pp. 1, 5a, 5b, 6, 7, 8a, 8b, 9, 10, 11, 12a, 12b, 13, 14a, 14b, 15a, 15b, 16, 17, 18a, 18b, 19, 20, 21, 22, 23a, 23b, 24, 25a, 25b, 26a, 26b, 27, 28, 29, 30c.

Cover photograph of Stephanos and friends, reproduced with permission of Fiona Freund. Many thanks to Stephanos, Dimitria, Chrysanna and their families.

Every effort has been made to contact copyright holders of any material reproduced in this book. Any omissions will be rectified in subsequent printings if notice is given to the publisher. The paper used to print this book comes from sustainable resources.

Some words are shown in bold, **like this**. You can find out what they mean by looking in the glossary.

Contents

Where Is Greece?

To learn about Greece we meet three children who live there. Greece is a country in Europe. It has a long **coast** and more that 2,000 islands.

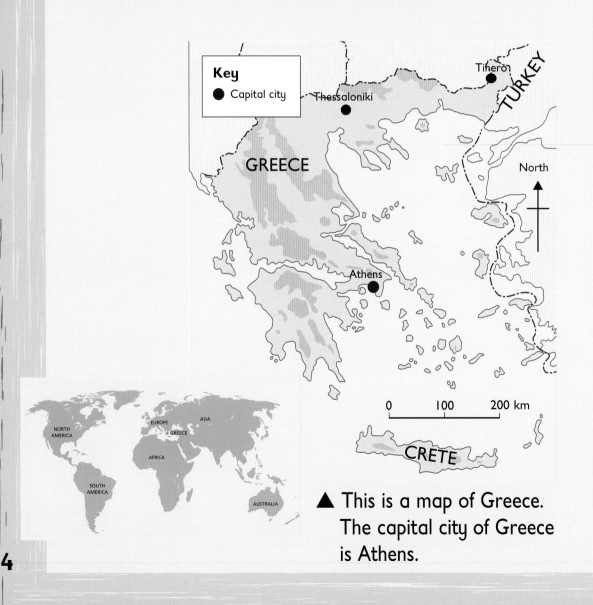

▲ This is a map of Greece. The capital city of Greece is Athens.

Greece has many hills and mountains.
It is sunny and hot for most of the
year. In the winter it rains. Sometimes
it even snows.

Meet Stefanos

Stefanos is seven years old. He comes from a city called Thessaloniki. He lives with his parents and his younger brother, Dimitris.

Stefanos's father is a business person. His mother runs a shop. The family lives in a modern apartment with a **balcony.**

Stefanos's mother

Stefanos's father

Stefanos

Dimitris

At School

Stefanos goes to school five days a week. School starts at 8.30 A.M. and ends at 1.30 P.M. His lessons are in Greek. He is starting to learn English, too.

8

At break, Stefanos loves playing basketball. He enjoys lots of sports, such as soccer and swimming.

What Is for Supper?

Stefanos's mother goes to the market to buy food. Thessaloniki is by the sea so the market has lots of fresh fish. It also sells fruit and vegetables that are grown in the countryside nearby.

Many Greek meals are made up of lots of small dishes, called *mezze*. Stefanos likes eating grape leaves stuffed with lamb and rice.

The Capital City

The capital city of Greece is Athens. It is in the southern part of the country. It is a very busy place because lots of people live there.

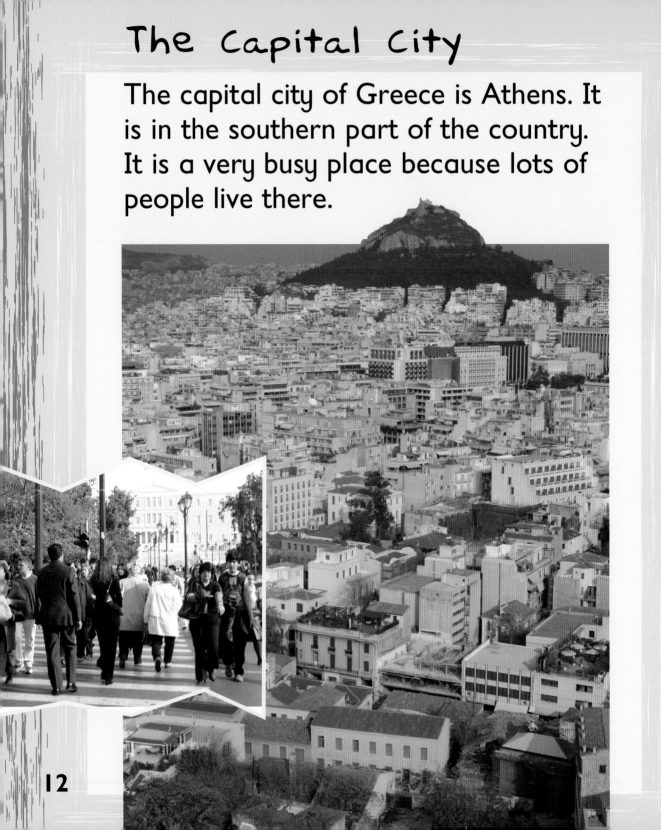

These soldiers are guarding the Greek **parliament** buildings in Athens. They are wearing the national costume. Greek people often wear the national costume at **festivals.**

Meet Dimitria

Dimitria is eight years old. She lives in a farming village in northern Greece. She lives with her parents and two older sisters.

Despina

Evangelia

Dimitria's father

Dimitria

Dimitria's mother

On their farm, Dimitria's family grows **sugar beets, cotton,** tomatoes, and watermelons. They also keep some chickens.

▼ Picking cotton is a messy business!

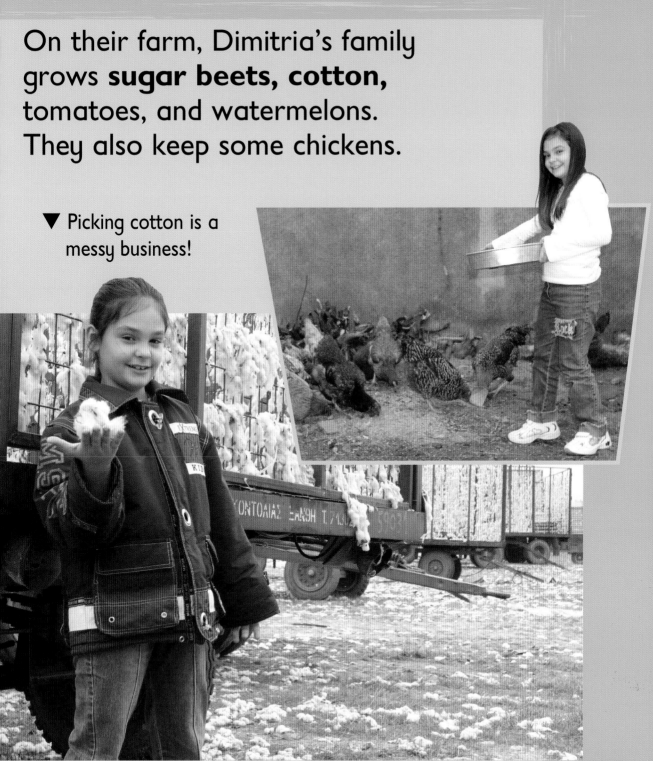

A Big Family

Dimitria's grandparents live near her. She sees them every day. Her grandmother taught her mother to make lace. Now Dimitria is learning, too.

Dimitria has lots of uncles, aunts and cousins who live nearby. They often see each other at big family meals.

▲ One uncle and aunt run a shop in the village.

Dimitria's Day

Dimitria goes to school five days a week. Every night she has three hours of homework. She also has jobs to do for her family.

▼ Dimitria helps take care of her grandmother's goats.

On Sundays, Dimitria goes to church.
She says prayers and lights a candle.
Afterward, her family goes out
together for a meal.

Boats and the Sea

There are all sorts of boats on the sea around Greece. Some are used for sailing or fishing. Some are used to move goods from place to place.

▼ These big ships are off the **coast** of Athens.

Many people who live on Greek islands have their own boats. It can be easier to travel by sea than to drive over the rocky land.

Meet Chrysanna

Chrysanna is eight years old. She lives with her parents and her three brothers. Chrysanna's family lives on a large Greek island called Crete.

Chrysanna's father

Nikolas

Chrysanna's mother

Epaminoudas

Orestis

Chrysanna

▲ Chrysanna's family is having lunch in a restaurant.

Chrysanna's family lives in an apartment in a seaside town. There are orange and **olive** trees near Chrysanna's home.

23

Summer by the Sea

Lots of people go to Crete for their summer vacations. Chrysanna's town is filled with small hotels, restaurants, and cafés.

Chrysanna's parents own a big hotel next to the beach. Chrysanna helps out when she does not have school.

Celebrations

Today, it is the name day of Chrysanna's best friend. This is the feast day of the **Christian saint** her friend is named after. Name days are even more important than birthdays!

▲ Time for a party!

At parties, people often do **traditional** dances to Greek music. Chrysanna and her friends are very good at traditional dancing. They learned it at school.

The History of Greece

The people who lived in Greece a long time ago are called the Ancient Greeks. They built many big, important cities. You can still see parts of them today.

▲ The Ancient Greeks made this building on a hill above Athens.

◄ The Ancient Greeks held plays in this outdoor theater.

The Ancient Greeks had many good ideas that we still use today. We often copy their rules, their buildings, their stories, their plays, and lots more!

Greek Fact File

Flag   **Capital City**   **Money**

Athens

Euros

Religion
• Most Greeks are **Orthodox Christians**. There are a few Muslims, too.

Language
• The language used in Greece is called Greek. It has a different alphabet from English. The Greek alphabet only has 24 letters.

Try speaking Greek!
These Greek words are written the way they sound:

yasoo .... *hello or goodbye*
parakalo .... *please*
tee kanees .... *how are you?*

Glossary

balcony floor on the outside of a building usually with a wall or rail around it

Christian saint a holy person in the Christian religion

coast where the land meets the sea

cotton a plant that can be made into cloth

festival big celebration for a town or country

Orthodox Christian an Orthodox Christian strictly follows the rules and traditions of the Christian religion

parliament the group of people who run a country

sugar beet a plant that can be made into sugar

traditional something that has been going for a very long time without changing

More Books to Read

Foster, Leila Merrell. *Europe*. Chicago: Heinemann Library, 2002.

Britton, Tamara L. *Greece*. London: Checkerboard Books, 2000.

McDonald, Fiona. *Ancient Greece*. Boston: Kingfisher, 2002.

Index